"Jesus loves you"; "He'll never leave you nor forsake you". I had heard these verses from the Bible most of my life; understanding the truth of what they actually were saying was the most difficult. Sure, we say them, but do we really believe them?

This is a story of me, coming into my identity as a child of God. I have illustrated this book with prophetic pictures given to me by the Lord.

When I was nineteen years old, I received the gift of the Holy Spirit in a wonderful church among friends, who became family. The love of God was powerful and exciting and I was sure nothing would ever change that beautiful feeling. After a few years, there was a sense this sweet love was diminishing, as rules from the leaders crept in. Rules that made me think I needed to perform, in order for God to love me. I began receiving constant correction from the very ones I had come to love so dearly, and the feelings of disapproval fell on me like a thick blanket. I couldn't seem live up to the high expectations of performance and finally left the church, heartbroken.

I battled the fear for years, that God didn't love me anymore. And I carried a burden that I didn't "fit the mold" of what a Christian should look like. So I made the decision to put up the walls of my heart. I built a box in my mind and let no one else in. This imaginary box became the only place I felt safe with God. I prayed often, but my past haunted me and my thoughts reminded me that, "I wasn't doing it right," and I questioned "did He still love me?"

Years later, after experiencing a series of emotionally traumatic events in my life, I found myself in a very dark place. Everything seemed to be closing in around me, but somehow I knew God was my only answer. My problem was, I didn't know how to get back to that place where I knew His love was real.

Working up some serious courage, I went to church one Sunday morning. I snuck into the back and slid into closest chair. The speaker was sharing a very different message that caused my heart to leap in my chest. *God loves you right where you are and you cannot do anything to earn it.* I had never heard it spoken this way and I felt God's love sweep over me like a fresh wind.

I soon joined a small group where I was welcomed with open arms. Through those relationships, I began to see and experience the love of God like I had once known. Learning to trust again didn't come so easily. "Should I let down the walls I have built around my heart?" See, letting others into my world was scary but I knew I was on a journey, and I needed to keep going. I can remember at one meeting in particular sensing God's presence in such a tangible way that I felt the heaviness I had carried for years disappear. The power of love awakened my heart and the box I had built for my own safety, was gone. I sensed everything in me; my heart, my mind and my emotions were filled with a wonderful peace and rest.

I began to hear His voice again, and yes, He does speak to His children. I saw vivid images in my mind like nothing I had ever seen before. God was unfolding my story the way He saw me, as a child. I always loved painting and I sensed I was to paint the visions that were revealed to my heart. I was out of practice and had many excuses, but hope was birthed in my heart once again, and I started painting.

This is my story painted on the pages: a journey of revelation and renewal. A story of God's overwhelming love, and His longing to unite sons and daughters back to the heart of the Father.

LOVE'S GIFT

A Story of Revelation and Renewal

Dedicated to Tyanne Hoy

Thank you for your constant love and prayers,
That gently reminded me-
"I am a child of God."

LOVE'S GIFT

A Story of Revelation and Renewal

Written by

Vickie Bell and Gayelee Reynolds

Illustrations by

Vickie Bell

I was shocked when I found myself walking down a dark road. At once, I realized I was no longer a grown woman but a little girl, and I felt very alone. The darkness was great and closed in all around me, leaving me with a feeling of fear and despair. My world seemed to be falling in all around me and nothing seemed right. But, where could I go?

An old song starts to ring in my head *"The name of the Lord is a strong tower, the righteous run into it and they are saved."* It had been a long time since I heard this song, and I remember thinking to myself, "The righteous?" That certainly was not me, my life was in shambles and I had wandered so far from God. I began believing the lies that swirled around in my mind, and feeling condemned I gave up. But, where could I hide?

As I looked further down the road, I saw what appeared to be a very large tower. Something inside of me compelled me to keep walking down that road, and as I took the first step, I felt a peace sweep over me. I had nowhere else to go and in that moment of loneliness and despair, this somehow felt right.

Gazing up, I stood in awe of the massive tower in front of me. It was as tall as the eye could see and I felt very small standing before it. Looking at the tower brought back to mind the song that was running through my head only moments before. "The name of the Lord is a strong tower." At that moment, the presence of God surrounded me like a warm blanket, and the darkness began to lift.

"God's name is a place of protection,
good people can run there and are safe"
Proverbs 18:10 (The Message)

As I stand wrapped in His presence, I open my eyes and I see wings. They are massive and beautiful, the very sight of them take my breath away. I then begin to realize that the darkness wasn't what I thought it was at all. I had been hidden in the shadow of the wings of God the whole time. I didn't know it nor did I believe it, He, The Father, God, the Almighty was always there, shadowing me in His love. I began to think back to all those hard times and I realize, only God could have seen me through. This thought alone made my heart shudder with hope and joy.

"He will cover you with His feathers, and under His wings you will find refuge; His faithfulness will be your shield and rampart."
Psalm 91:4 (NIV)

Then, the Lord spoke. Yes, I heard God's voice! "Come, talk to Me like you did before." I reached my hands into the air, like a child begging to be picked up into the arms of love. And I simply ask, "Father, do you still love me?"

"My sheep hear My voice, and I know them, and they follow Me"
John 10:27 (NASB)

I hear His gentle words whisper to my heart, "Just let Me hold you. Come and rest in Me." In rest, an unexplainable peace and joy starts filling my heart and His love pours into me like a warm liquid substance. I had forgotten the power of this love. I had forgotten that perfect love casts out all fear. Hot tears of freedom begin to fall down my face and I feel in that moment as if I was being born again.

"For I am the Lord your God, who upholds your right hand, who says to you, "Do not fear, I will help you."
Isaiah 41:13 (NASB)

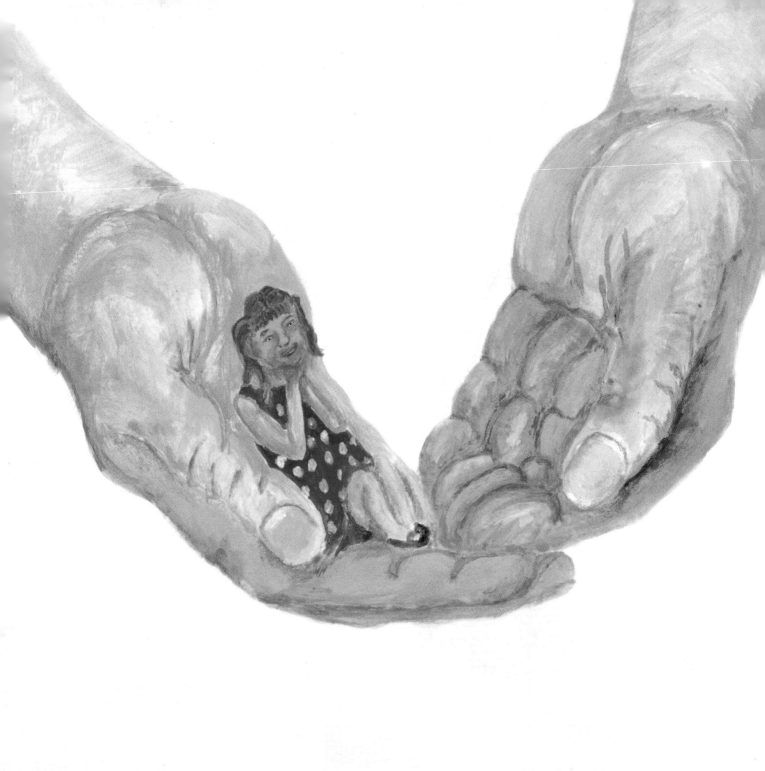

I hear Him say, "I have a very special gift for you my child."
There before me is a box, wrapped in the most beautiful paper adorned with a gold shiny bow. My heart begins to dance in my chest and a smile radiates on my face. I did nothing to deserve this gift for I have found delight in my Father's eyes.

I pull the beautiful gold bow free from the gift and open the box.
Inside was a jump rope? I wonder to myself, what kind of gift is this?
I hear His still small voice speak to me again, "You are my child. Jump,
play and have fun in my presence."

"Truly, I say to you, unless you turn and become like children,
you will never enter the kingdom of heaven.
Whoever humbles himself like this child
is the greatest in the kingdom of heaven.
Matthew 18:2-4 (ESV)

I had forgotten what it was like to have fun! I grabbed the jump rope from inside the box and I begin to jump and jump and jump. As the rope went faster and faster, the laughter came out of my belly like gushing rivers that had been locked up for a long time. The joy of the Lord is my strength and at that moment, I felt like the strongest girl alive.

Jumping faster and laughing out loud, I noticed angels all around me. They too, were jumping and laughing with me. Heaven was having a party and I was invited. This was so wonderful! I didn't feel alone and it seemed like God sent Heaven to Earth, to show me that He was very close.

"For He will command His angels concerning you
to guard you in all your ways."
Psalm 91:11 (NIV)

As I was jumping, I begin to think of all the junk that was in my heart. I had let so many bad thoughts come into my mind, which caused a lot of ugliness to come from my heart. I prayed, "Abba, please take my ugly heart, I've really messed it up... can you fix it?" And, I waited.

"I will give you a new heart and put a new spirit in you;
I will remove from you your heart of stone and give you a heart of flesh."
Ezekiel 36:26 (NASB)

As soon as I said the words, He was already handing me a new heart.
I was astounded. All the darkness was gone. All the pain, the mistakes, all the things that I thought made me bad, and made God reject me were all gone.

The gentle healing hands of Father God, had touched my heart with such precision. His love filled my darkness and everything appeared so bright. I was overwhelmed as tears of gladness ran down my face. A little girl crying with joy as all the noise inside of me stopped.

I begin to say, "Thank You," over and over again.
God's love had taken away my darkness and made my heart begin to dance again.

"You have turned my mourning into joyful dancing.
You have taken away my clothes of mourning and clothed me with joy."
Psalm 30:11

The joy and hope inside of me was so overwhelming. His love began spilling out of me like rivers of water. Splashes of love were everywhere I stepped. I wanted to; I had to share this life changing experience everywhere I went. God's love has become rain for dry and weary hearts and it is there for all to taste and see. I learned that the Father withholds no good thing from his sons and daughters. He longs to lavish us with His extravagant love.

"And this hope will not lead to disappointment. For we know how dearly God loves us, because He has given us the Holy Spirit to fill our hearts with His love.
Romans 5:5 (NLT)

It was time to head down the path again; the road was no longer dark. There were beautiful flowing green fields and flowers all around me. I had an overwhelming sense of awe. He isn't just my God. He isn't just my Lord. He had become my Abba, my daddy. The closeness I felt was like no other experience I had ever encountered. He had become my safe place, my strong tower and a love that I had never known before. I hear His still small voice one more time. "Hold my hand and I will lead you."

The Lord is my shepherd;
I have all that I need.
He lets me rest in green meadows;
He leads me beside peaceful streams.
He renews my strength.
He guides me along right paths,
bringing honor to his name.
Even when I walk through the darkest valley,
I will not be afraid, for you are close beside me.

Psalm 23:1-4 NLT